Rachel

Maddow

A Biography Prequel Exploring American Democracy And The Fight Against The Threat Of Fascism.

Bobby Brandy

Table Of Content

A concise short read

Introduction

Rachel Maddow is a popular political commentator and television host known for her outspoken liberal views. She is the host of the highly successful television show, "The Rachel Maddow Show," which has made her a prominent voice in both radio and television.

Even as a child, Maddow was inquisitive, confident, and full of energy. At the age of seven, she was already reading the newspaper cover to cover and engaging in critical analysis by asking questions about what she read. Maddow's broadcasting career started on the radio, when she aired a show on WRNX in Holyoke, Massachusetts. She eventually joined Air America Radio and, after presenting and co-hosting several episodes, her own show, 'The Rachel Maddow Show,' was broadcast. Because of the success of this show, a television show of the same name was shown on MSNBC. Rachel fully acknowledged her sexuality and is the first lesbian anchor to headline a major prime-time news show in the United States.

She has been in the vanguard of spreading the liberal agenda since her debut on her Air America talk show in 2005, courageously and unerringly discussing local and worldwide problems affecting the US. Her show is well-known for its in-depth analysis of current events, political commentary, and interviews with celebrities.

A Brief Biography

Rachel Maddow was born in Castro Valley, California, on July 1, 1973, to an Air Force captain father and a mother who ran a school program and wrote for the local newspaper. Her family had a diverse heritage, with ancestors from the Netherlands, Canada, and what is now Ukraine and Lithuania. Maddow was raised in a highly conservative Catholic community. As a child, she was exposed to a variety of perspectives and experiences that would shape her worldview and political beliefs later in life. Maddow was a talented scholar as a youngster. According to her parents, she taught herself to read by the age of four. She was also a standout athlete in high school, participating in volleyball, basketball, and swimming. However, a shoulder injury in her final year caused her to reconsider a future in sports. She had the opportunity to receive a sports scholarship, but she chose not to combat her ailments.

Rachel was raised in a community where being homosexual was frowned upon. In Castro Valley, homophobia and bigotry were the order of the day. Maddow had empathy for homosexual people long before she realized she was gay. Rachel discovered she was homosexual after enrolling at Stanford University. At Stanford, she realized that no one in her 1000-person class had come out as homosexual. Rachel then decided to carry out an interview with one of her friends who was also coming out for the student newspaper. She had not yet come out to her parents at this point.

Maddow intended to inform her parents the weekend before the paper was due to be published. The article, however, was published before the weekend, and the news got to her parents before she could notify them. Rachel's family found the news difficult to accept at first. Her parents were particularly upset since her sexuality contradicted their Catholic beliefs. Over time, they finally came to accept her as she was.

After graduating from Stanford with a degree in Public Policy, Rachel was awarded a Rhodes scholarship to continue her postgraduate studies at Lincoln College. She lived in Lincoln until 1999, when she returned to the United States to complete her thesis.

To support herself financially, Rachel worked a variety of odd jobs in Massachusetts while writing her thesis. One of those jobs led her to meet Susan Mikula, a photographer who was in the process of renovating a run-down property. They began dating, and Rachel eventually received her PhD in Politics from Oxford University in 2001. Rachel was diagnosed with cyclical depression at the age of 12, a condition that she has had to cope with throughout her life. While the depression does not diminish the satisfaction she finds in her work or in being her authentic self, it is a challenge that she faces on an ongoing basis. Despite these challenges, Rachel has remained resilient and focused on her goals.

Rachel's distinctive style and perspective quickly made her a fan favorite after she made her television debut. People appreciated her for being a prominent LGBTQ+ figure in the media landscape, and for presenting a different perspective than the typical television host. Her popularity has soared among the left, who view her as a powerful voice in the resistance to the Trump administration. However, her popularity among the far-right has diminished as a result of her strong opposition to Trump's policies.

Rachel became deeply involved in the fight against AIDS, many years after the initial cases were reported. Living in San Francisco, she had seen firsthand the devastating impact of the virus on her community.

While studying at Oxford, she volunteered for an AIDS charity, and her dissertation focused on AIDS and health care reform in American and British prisons. She was so concerned about the issue that she put her political ambitions on hold in order to focus on the AIDS crisis. Rachel made the transition from radio to cable television in 2006, when she began regularly appearing on "The Situation with Tucker Carlson" on MSNBC. During the 2006 midterm elections, she was also a frequent guest on CNN's "Paula Zahn Now." These television appearances helped to raise her profile and establish her as a respected player in the field.

In 2008, Rachel Maddow was hired by MSNBC as a political commentator, and she quickly rose to prominence as the network's most visible personality. She was known for her liberal views and for championing progressive ideas on her show, which became a hit with viewers. As the political divide on cable news became more pronounced, Maddow became a key voice for the liberal perspective.

Rachel has been recognized for her news coverage with a number of awards, including an Emmy Award for her episode "Good Morning Landlocked Central Asia" on "The Rachel Maddow Show," as well as the Gracie Award from American Women in Radio and Television in 2009. She also received the Maggie Award in 2010 for her coverage of healthcare reforms and the anti-abortion movement, especially the murder of Dr. George Tiller. That same year, she also received the Walter Cronkite Faith and

Freedom Award for her documentary 'The Assassination of Dr. Tiller'. In addition to her Emmy and Gracie Awards, Rachel has also received the John Steinbeck Award from San Jose State University, as well as the GLAAD Award for outstanding journalism. In 2012, she was named to TIME magazine's "TIME 100" list, which recognizes the most influential people in the world. Rachel has also received the prestigious Edward R. Murrow Award for her excellence in electronic journalism.

Literary Works

Maddow has written many books in addition to her television show. Her works often deal with politics, international policy, and corporate power. She is widely acknowledged as one of the most important characters in American media, and her television show and comments have had a tremendous effect on political dialogue.

The Drift

Those picking up Rachel Maddow's debut book might expect a humorous leftist critique of the military. Instead, they'll find a spirited but serious argument about American history. Maddow brings her trademark intelligence, humor, and passion to her arguments, but always with a strong grounding in facts. Her analysis is thoughtful and nuanced, making the book a must-read for anyone interested in American politics and history.

If the book entices readers to leave their political silos for a moment, it will be because Maddow's premise spans ideological borders. She is of the opinion that the United States must revert to the founding ideals of the country, in her instance a distrust of standing militaries and a genuine aversion to war. "Drift" is a fascinating and shocking look at the misadventures and missteps of the U.S. military since World War II. From botched missions to accidental nuclear mishaps, Maddow chronicles the often-bizarre history of American military interventionism.

From the bizarre invasion of Grenada to the ill-fated Fallujah sewage plant, Maddow reveals the absurdities and tragedies of America's post-WWII military engagements. These are tales of people who did not need to die in wars that did not need to be waged. What's striking about these misadventures is not so much the ineffectiveness or institutional overreach of military leaders, but rather the willingness of the last five presidents to radically expand the military's role for their own political and ideological purposes. As a result, we have seen a kind of perpetual conflict, with no clear end in sight. Maddow's book provides a compelling critique of the role of the military in U.S. foreign policy and the costs of this perpetual conflict.

Congress is chastised for abdicating its constitutionally mandated role to authorize and support war, but Maddow singles out Presidents Ronald Reagan, George Bush I, Bill Clinton, George Bush II, and Barack Obama. Each devised new techniques to get around Congress and overcome popular disapproval. The book catalogs a litany of tactics that have been used to expand the military's role in American life: the use of private contractors in place of a reserve force, making it easier to wage war without the public feeling the full impact; the expansion of secrecy under the guise of intelligence operations, making it more difficult to hold the government accountable; and the elevation of military leaders to the role of deciding not just how to go to war, but whether to do so in the first place.

In "Drift," Rachel Maddow explores how the feel-good, feel-strong messages of Reagan-era propaganda have become normalized in American society. Air Force flyovers at football games, TV ads featuring young people signing up for military service, and images of smart missiles hitting their targets have become so commonplace that we barely even notice them anymore. But these images have had a profound impact on our collective psyche, making it easier to accept and even support military action.

The Pentagon's annual advertising budget of $600 million has been used to shape public opinion and support for military action, with little more than a salute and a mortgaged future required in return. According to Maddow, these images have made international affairs and the Constitution largely irrelevant in discussions about the use of military force. In this new order, the military is elevated to the status of a "super-citizen," while ordinary citizens are reduced to mere spectators.

While Maddow does an excellent job of criticizing the increased use of military contractors, she doesn't fully acknowledge the role that these companies have played in shaping the current state of affairs. For example, the military contractor Lockheed Martin has received annual military contracts that are larger than the combined budgets of several major government agencies. This level of funding gives the contractors significant influence over policy decisions, and it's worth considering whether their influence has played a role in perpetuating the need for war. Maddow's message is one that the nation needs to hear, perhaps more than any other: the increasing reliance on military force poses a significant threat to our freedoms and way of life. A democracy requires multiple voices to be involved in the decision to use force, in order to avoid rash and unnecessary wars. Unless we reverse the loss of civilian control over the military, we will continue to have a government that is constantly at war.

According to Maddow, the decision to go to war has become far too easy in recent decades, and this has had serious consequences. Congress's constitutional authority to declare war has been largely ignored, and the consequences of war are felt by only a small percentage of the population. This lack of widespread awareness allows many Americans to remain blissfully ignorant of the human cost of war.

The military's growing reliance on contractors to provide combat support has had a profound impact on the way wars are fought. This privatization of military functions has created a lucrative security industry that benefits from the continued state of war, and which uses its influence to maintain the support of compliant members of Congress. Today's wars are often fought remotely, using robotic drones that allow soldiers to remain physically safe, even as they carry out lethal operations. Maddow's compelling narrative may lead readers to overlook some of the flaws in her argument. For example, while it's true that Congress authorized the wars in Afghanistan and Iraq, many have questioned the extent to which this authorization was based on faulty or incomplete information.

Similarly, while it's true that civilian casualties from drone strikes in Pakistan are lower than those that might result from a conventional war, this doesn't address the ethical and legal issues raised by drone warfare. Maddow's "Drift" is a thought-provoking and engaging book that resonates with readers from a variety of political backgrounds. One of the most compelling practical solutions proposed in the book is the idea of raising taxes or selling war bonds to fund any military conflict, since the costs of war should be felt by the entire nation from the outset. This would create a powerful incentive to avoid unnecessary military interventions and to consider the consequences of war more carefully.

The Bag Man

One of the core principles of democracy is that the law applies equally to everyone, regardless of their position or power. However, this principle has often been violated by political leaders who have escaped accountability for their misconduct, especially in recent times. For example, President Gerald Ford granted a pardon to Richard Nixon after he resigned over the Watergate scandal in 1974, and Nixon never faced any legal consequences. Similarly, President George H.W. Bush pardoned six of his aides who were involved in the

Iran-contra affair in the final days of his term in 1992. Moreover, the Justice Department rules that were in place during the Watergate era prevented special counsel Robert Mueller from charging President Trump with obstruction of justice.

In their book "Bag Man", based on their popular podcast of the same name, Rachel Maddow and Michael Yarvitz present a case study of how the democratic ideal of equal justice under the law clashes with the grim reality of America's political system. They offer a lively and compelling narrative of the attempt to hold Vice President Spiro Agnew criminally responsible, and they expose the legal, moral, and political difficulties of bringing presidents and vice presidents to justice. Many media personalities tend to favor historical narratives that are based on unfounded conspiracy theories or are infused with nationalistic sentiments. In contrast, Maddow and Yarvitz adopt a more rigorous and insightful approach, drawing on archival sources and oral histories to uncover new details about the challenges that prosecutors faced when they investigated Agnew's abuse of power.

A group of young prosecutors, led by U.S. Attorney George Beall, discovered evidence of corruption involving Vice President Spiro Agnew's previous roles in Baltimore County and Maryland. The prosecutors found that

Agnew had received kickbacks from construction firms in return for government contracts. Attorney General Elliot Richardson backed the prosecutors' efforts to pursue and indict Agnew, even though it put him in conflict with the Nixon administration. The prosecutors' commitment and Richardson's support eventually resulted in Agnew's resignation from office.

However, bringing the case to trial was not an easy task. The principle that no one is above the law collided with the authority of Agnew's office, the partisan politics, and the escalating Watergate crisis. Beall's brother, a Republican senator from Maryland, joined Republican National Committee Chairman

George Bush and other GOP leaders in pressuring the Justice Department to ease its stance on the investigation. The prosecutors stood their ground.

Agnew publicly denied any wrongdoing and claimed that he was a victim of a witch hunt, orchestrated by a liberal media that wanted to destroy a leader who challenged the political establishment. Richardson was most concerned about Watergate because it endangered Nixon's presidency; if Nixon resigned or was impeached, allowing Agnew to become president while he was under investigation for bribery would plunge the nation into another crisis. Lawyers in the Justice Department faced a dilemma: how to uphold the law and serve the nation's best interests? Richardson decided to strike a bargain with Agnew's lawyers: Agnew would avoid jail time and criminal charges by pleading no contest to tax fraud and resigning as vice president. This was preferable to risking him becoming president if he faced a trial for his abuse of power.

'Bag Man' depicts Agnew as a precursor of Trump's divisive and destructive politics. Agnew used cultural resentment to galvanize the loyal support of a growing White working-class Republican base, attacking liberal politicians as radical leftists and TV journalists as paranoid alarmists. The vice president's rhetoric made him a national lightning rod. However, Agnew and Trump were not identical, and neither were their political contexts. 'Bag Man' may exaggerate Agnew's individual impact, while ignoring the role of other influential figures such as Joe McCarthy, Roy Cohn, George Wallace, Phyllis Schlafly and Newt Gingrich.

Moreover, the emergence of the far-right media and grassroots conservative activism in the 1970s and 1980s created a political environment that was already receptive to Trump's style of politics. The book claims that Beall took all the heat while resisting pressure to let Agnew off the hook. Maddow and Yarvitz recount Frank Sinatra's contribution to Agnew's legal defense fund after the vice president shielded Sinatra from allegations of mafia ties, remarking that the singer returned the favor, Ocean's-11 style.

"Bag Man" also favors a black-and-white narrative, which lacks nuance and reveals the shortcomings of converting partisan cable TV and podcasts into serious historical inquiry. One of the prosecutors called Agnew pure evil in the book, which fails to explain how someone who could ascend to the vice presidency would also engage in such a prolonged criminal scheme or the sources that sustained Agnew's strong political support. Nevertheless, this engaging and well-documented book exposes how the country's judicial and political institutions fail to hold the nation's highest elected officials accountable for their crimes. Agnew eventually resigned. He, like Nixon, never went to prison and never faced trial. He continued to pollute the public sphere by publishing a conspiracy-ridden and anti-Semitic book, and he spent his days without ever confronting the full consequences of his years of betraying public trust.

The Blowout

The book "Blowout" exposes the dark side of the fossil fuel industry, which the author calls the devil's dung. The author does not mince words or present a balanced perspective. She states her thesis clearly: "The oil and gas industry is the most consequential, lucrative, powerful, and poorly governed major industry in human history."

The book focuses on two countries, the United States and Russia, and how they have been corrupted and manipulated by a greedy fossil fuel sector, both individually and collectively. The author argues that the industry is behind almost everything that happens in the world. It is a key factor in the current global instability and democratic decline. The industry is so rich, so huge, so intertwined with every aspect of our lives and the lives of everyone on the planet that, if you follow the links, it reveals how practically everything in the world works — and, she warns, it will eventually destroy the whole freaking planet.

The title of the book refers to the horrifying moment when pressure in an oil or gas well builds up and control systems fail, causing the fuel to surge back up to the rig and explode in a fireball. "Blowout" reads like one of Maddow's MSNBC rants, with anger piled on top of indignation and frantic digressions warning of Armageddon. You can almost picture her making her point with a finger jab.

Maddow's story connects fracking in Oklahoma, Russian sleeper agents, the depraved son of Equatorial Guinea's president, earthquake clusters, poisoned pets, the hacker Guccifer, the killing of Moammar Gaddafi, a separatist movement in Texas, and more. According to Maddow, fossil fuels are the world's cheap high, a global addiction that produces such enormous, immediate, effortless profits for connected elites that no one wants to do anything but chase the oil jackpot. Teodoro Nguema Obiang Mangue, the rogue son of Equatorial Guinea's president-for-life Teodoro Obiang Nguema Mbasogo, is one of the more extreme examples. He lived in a $30 million mansion in Malibu, California, and had properties all over the world, a collection of luxury cars, and a large yacht.

He liked to spoil his girlfriends with a shopping spree by giving her $80,000 in $100 bills from a Nike shoe box stuffed with cash. Oil was discovered off the shore, and as a result, a Global Witness report shows, the small country's oil revenues rose from $2.1 million in 1993 to $3.9 billion in 2007. Meanwhile, 77 percent of the people were poor. Maddow began tracing the industry and its impact on our lives in 1859, with the discovery of rock oil and, a few years later, the establishment of Standard Oil by John D. Rockefeller. She updates the story with modern innovations like hydraulic fracturing and horizontal drilling, which have transformed extraction and helped push America toward energy independence.

The federal and state tax breaks for the industry, which Maddow calls the nation's longest-running welfare program, are inseparably linked to America's fossil fuel legacy. As a result, the fossil fuel sector began to prey on the body politic, eventually creating its own corporate shadow foreign policy. The ultimate victims, according to Maddow, are ordinary Americans across the country who are trapped by an industry that gives them jobs while endangering their health and even their lives, all while undermining democracy.

Russia, which has strong democratic institutions, fared much worse, afflicted by the Resource Curse – abundant energy resources that generate huge financial flows but crowd out more sustainable and diverse economic development paths. As a result, weak governance and high corruption levels have devastating economic, health, and environmental consequences at the local level, as well as a high frequency of conflict and war. The book is full of unsavory characters, but there are also a few heroes. One of them is Austin Holland, the chief seismologist at the Oklahoma Geological Survey, who, despite intense pressure from the oil and gas industry and its allies, persisted in his research and uncovered a connection between wastewater disposal from fracking and a dramatic rise in earthquakes in the state.

He ultimately left his job and moved to New Mexico to work for the U.S. Geological Survey. In the face of tremendous adversity, Holland stood up for science and public safety. For Maddow, the real heroes are the Oklahoma teachers, students, and parents who spoke out against the negative effects of fracking, including frequent earthquakes, and tax breaks for the oil and gas industry, while school funding was severely cut. They took action and pushed for a change, and eventually the state government increased taxes on the industry and tightened regulations on wastewater disposal. Their determination to improve their communities despite facing incredible obstacles is truly inspiring.

While the fossil fuel industry is not going away overnight, Maddow argues that it is a dying industry that will eventually fade away. She argues that the world must work towards a future without fossil fuels, despite the environmental and geopolitical damage that the industry has caused. Despite the immense challenges that lie ahead, she maintains that a better future is possible, and that change can begin right here at home.

The Prequel

How could thousands of Americans gather at Madison Square Garden in 1939 under a portrait of George Washington to support the Nazis? This is one of the shocking stories that Rachel Maddow uncovered in her years of research for her book, "Prequel." It's a warning tale about the threats to democracy during WWII. Maddow reveals that many Americans not only opposed the US involvement in the war, but also sided with the Nazis. She first explored this topic in a podcast series called "Ultra," which examined the strange connections between

Americans and Nazi agendas. Some of the most alarming stories Maddow shares are about a nationwide network of secret pro-Nazi, anti-Semitic groups, such as the Silver Shirts, exposed by Arnold Eric Sevareid, a young reporter who later became a famous CBS News correspondent.

He found out that there was a band of extreme right-wing fanatics who met covertly in Minneapolis. They were forming armed militias across the country to wage war against the Jews and establish a Hitler-like dictatorship here. Sevareid infiltrated this organization and realized that they were not only crazy, but also dangerous. The Christian Front, another anti-Semitic militia, used the

165th Regiment Armory on Lexington Avenue in New York City as a storage facility for weapons and explosives. Maddow says that they had an insider captain in the 165th Infantry Regiment who was ready to supply them with ammunition, cordite, and hand grenade materials. They also stored explosives there.

The FBI arrested them in mid-January 1940. The FBI believed they were only a week away from executing the Christian Front's plan to assassinate several Congressmen and fire bomb various New York City sites that they thought would trigger a racial war. Eighteen defendants were charged with seditious conspiracy and theft of government property. And they walked free. All of them got either a hung jury or an acquittal. The public reaction was, 'Oh, it was a Brooklyn verdict for these Brooklyn boys,' and they were treated as local heroes. Their fierce anti-Semitism, even violent, was seen as a kind of patriotic anti-communism.

Before the internet became a source of misinformation, the Harmonie Club - the second-oldest private club in New York City, exclusively for Jews who were excluded from other private clubs - was accused of a sinister plot to harm Jews. Some shady characters, including a former Army general, told a Congressional committee in 1939 that they had discovered a conspiracy being hatched at the Harmonie Club involving prominent Jews linked to the Roosevelt administration, such as Supreme Court Justice Felix Frankfurter and Treasury Secretary Henry Morgenthau.

Maddow reveals how the newly established House Un-American Activities Committee received a report from two witnesses about the Harmonie Club. They testified before Congress that the Jews were plotting to overthrow the United States and establish their own rule, and that they were there to expose this conspiracy. According to Maddow, this was a fabricated story. It was part of an effort to influence Americans to adopt Hitler's anti-Semitic views. Hitler had many agents in the United States, one of them being George Sylvester Vierek, who lived in a luxurious ten-room apartment on Riverside Drive in New York City. He was very rich, as he was the most senior and highest-paid Nazi propagandist in the United States.

Vierek had been a spy during World War I and was convicted of espionage, but he escaped on legal technicalities and went on to lead an operation linked to Capitol Hill. Maddow explains that they would smuggle Nazi propaganda into the United States and persuade a congressman or a senator to endorse it and put it in the Congressional Record. Once it was there, they could distribute it widely across the country. Maddow accuses Senators Ernest Lundeen of Minnesota and Burton Wheeler of Montana, as well as Representative Hamilton Fish III of New York, of collaborating with Vierek during WWII. However, when the federal government finally indicted nearly two dozen people for sedition, including Vierek and several congressional staffers, none of the congressmen were prosecuted.

The congressmen who were involved in this scheme exerted a lot of pressure on the Justice Department. The case also fell apart. Maddow describes the trial as a circus, a mess, and a disaster. The prosecution had a strong case. But then, seven months into the trial, the judge died. U.S. District Judge Edward Clayton Eicher, 65, passed away after a heart attack. After several years of consideration, the Justice Department decided not to retry the case. As the attack on Pearl Harbor brought the United States into the war, the American people shifted their attention to the war rather than the domestic conflict.

Maddow's book is set three-quarters of a century ago, but it has a reason to be called "Prequel." It was written in the wake of the assault on the U.S. Capitol. She believes that what we are witnessing now is a new version of the far-right. And it has some of the most alarming features that indicate a democracy that is at risk of falling to authoritarianism. Violence is penetrating the political sphere. Minorities are being scapegoated, and harmful conspiracy theories are being promoted. Rising anti-Semitism is a major red flag. Anti-Semitism often goes hand in hand with an increase in fascist tendencies. And it's something we can't afford to overlook.

She contended that there is a history here that we should learn from. Americans before us fought such battles, and they were just as brilliant, resourceful, witty, and clear-headed as any of us could aspire to be. We can learn from their actions.

Fascism And American Democracy

Fascist ideologies gained popularity in the 1930s. This was mirrored in the rapid expansion of Nazi groups. Ku Klux Klan gatherings were regular and widespread; Trump's father was allegedly detained at one such event while dressed in Klan garb. According to a 1941 publication, more than 100 similar groups had been established since 1933. Fascist beliefs had an appeal that reached well beyond the fringe, reaching important people such as Henry Ford and Charles Lindbergh. Lindbergh even went so far as to call Adolf Hitler a "great man."

Lindbergh's wife released a best-seller in 1940, calling authoritarianism "The Wave of the Future" and an ultimately positive view of mankind.

At the time, Jews played the same role for American fascists that immigrants, Muslims, and other minorities do today: a nebulous but wicked danger to America's grandeur. Surveys of public opinion in the United States from the 1930s provide a surprising reminder of how common these ideas grew. As late as July 1942, a Gallup survey would show that one in six Americans believed Hitler was doing the right thing to the Jews. According to a 1940 study, roughly one-fifth of Americans, including Germans, considered Jews as a national threat. Almost a third expected a broad anti-Jewish campaign, which 12 percent of Americans were ready to accept.

The anti-Semitic views of prominent figures like Catholic priest Charles Coughlin demonstrated the appeal of fascist ideologies to a large segment of the American public in the 1930s. Coughlin's radio program had a massive audience, and he often praised Nazi Germany and its policies. He would later break with President Roosevelt in 1934 and eventually be silenced in 1942, demonstrating the limits of his political power. These were not marginal extremists, but mainstream intellectuals, leaders of large organizations, and editors of popular magazines who embraced fascism. The president of the American Political Science Association — the oldest and largest organization of political scientists in the nation — denounced the doctrine of universal suffrage in his 1934 presidential address, arguing for the elimination of a democracy that allowed the ignorant, uninformed, and antisocial elements to vote.

If these changes smelled of fascism, he reasoned, we would have already recognized that there is a significant part of fascist theory and practice that we must adopt. The key elements that fueled the growth of fascism in America at the time are still relevant now.

The first was a severe economic downturn and social upheaval, which eroded people's trust in democracy and drove them to seek alternatives. As a US economist observed in 1933, democracy is neither expert nor fast to act, making it difficult to address group and class issues.

The fear of communism prompted many prominent intellectuals to adopt fascism as a defense against Bolshevism and as a lesser evil. As in Europe, concerns about communism enhanced fascism's allure in the U.S. Another factor was the emergence of Nazi Germany as an economic and military force. Hitler's rise initiated a long phase of German recovery, economic growth and the rapid elimination of unemployment in that country. By 1939, Germany faced a labor shortage of 2 million people, while industrial output had more than doubled. Historians have argued for generations whether the recovery was genuine, but the general impression of German success drew admirers regardless of its truth.

Even if these three causes are no longer present, comparable issues lay under the surface of current political life, flaws that may potentially fuel a rebirth of fascist groups. The general economy of the United States is doing well, but inequality is increasing. Widespread unemployment and a major drug pandemic have engulfed much of

America. These are the kinds of economic circumstances that fueled fascist support in the 1930s. Another significant catastrophe, such as the Great Recession, is likely to strengthen nationalist sentiments even more.

Today, few people are concerned about the communist menace. However, fear of communism has given way to the dread of globalists and elite technocrats who allegedly strive to destroy and control average Americans' lives.

Conclusion

In the twentieth century, democracy spread from a handful of isolated enclaves to nearly every corner of the globe. For those who have grown up with its values of freedom and prosperity, democracy's superiority seems self-evident. However, history has shown that moral appeal alone is often not enough to ensure the survival of democracy. To view democracy's success as a simple morality tale - the inevitable triumph of good over evil - would be a comforting but potentially dangerous mistake. For most of the twentieth century, the spread of democracy was aided by the presence of powerful nations such as the United States, which served as a model for others to follow. The promise of economic prosperity and political stability was a more powerful motivator for the spread of democracy than any abstract ideal of freedom.

However, as demonstrated by the shift in public and elite opinion during the Great Depression, democracy is vulnerable to erosion when it fails to deliver on its promises. The battle to defend American democracy in the face of fascism's mounting menace is long and tough, but it is not without hope. We can maintain the strength and resilience of our democracy by adhering to our basic beliefs and committing to the preservation of our institutions. The path ahead may be difficult, but if we stay consistent in our defense of democracy, we can defeat the menace of fascism and assure a better future for our country. Never underestimate the value of our democratic principles or the power of our democratic institutions.

Let us recall Abraham Lincoln's words: 'The life of a country is safe only while the nation is honest, truthful, and moral.' We must endeavor to live up to these values in our battle to maintain American democracy and resist fascism.

Appreciation

Thank you for choosing to read this book and for taking the time to learn about the life and work of Rachel Maddow. I would like to express my deepest gratitude for your interest and support. Your engagement with this work is a testament to the importance of understanding the challenges facing American democracy and the need to confront the threat of fascism.

Together, we can make a difference.

For further reading, I recommend Rachel Maddow's book Prequel: An American Fight Against Fascism. You can find it on Amazon.

The End

Made in United States
Troutdale, OR
11/29/2023

15120436R00040